GOLDEN THREADS.

BEAUTIFUL TRAITOR BOOKS

GOLDEN THREADS

Words for every day, every heart

KINGSLEY L. DENNIS

Copyright © 2019 by Kingsley L. Dennis

All rights reserved. No part of this work may be reproduced or transmitted in any form or by any means, electronic or mechanical, including photocopying and recording, or by any information storage or retrieval system without the prior written permission of Beautiful Traitor Books.

Published by Beautiful Traitor Books –
http://www.beautifultraitorbooks.com/

Any person who does any unauthorized act in relation to this publication may be liable to criminal prosecution and civil claims for damages. The author has asserted his right to be identified as the author of this work in accordance with the Copyright, Design and Patents Act 1988.

ISBN-13:   978-1-9993440-2-3   (paperback)

First published: 2019

Front Cover & Book Design – Ibolya Kapta

Original golden thread image by Naomi Hasegawa (used with permission).
For more information: www.naomihasegawa.com

1

If the outer sun rises
but the inner sun does not,

then nothing has been gained.

Only those who take the first step

can learn to walk.

First meetings never come again
no matter how hard
you wish for them.

They are precious,
like a
jewelled kiss.

Not everyone who arrives will stay.

Not everyone
who stays

has arrived.

Nothing in this world

is without its

rhyme or reason.

We gather and collect things
 - but not for ourselves.

We are not keepers.
We collect in order to give away.

Do you understand
what that means?

What we do here is
not for ourselves.

But in doing so,
we also help ourselves.

This is how *we* understand the world.

8

A generous heart
always seeks
to re-establish
harmony.

Seek the joyful,
unobtrusive moments
where life is like an older girl
that takes your hand
and guides you into play.

In such moments,
life hides the veils
of sorrow;

of scars

and of

suffering.

Freedom within

is the freedom

we can share with others.

If we do not educate ourselves,
we cannot be educated for the world.

We all arrive here as little ones,
dependent and incomplete.

We must earn our independence,
and work towards our completion.

Learning never stops
— it is like a river that
flows endlessly.

It shall take us through our whole life,
accompanying us through all our years,

like the fruit that hangs from the tree,
or the flowers that
bend in the breeze.

And like all living things, it contains within it
the inner longing to understand more
— to grow in mindfulness,
gratitude, and appreciation.

It is a world that opens up within
and inspires you to go forth with
a great energy and trust,
and with the incalculable sense of wonder.

Everything
is a wonder.

When we listen to our bodies
we are listening also
to our larger mind.

The mind is not only in the head
but is in the
whole body.

It listens to us.

14

Supreme self-discipline

is the same

as sincere surrender.

Unless you are able to do a thing,
you will not be able
to understand
the *why* of it.

The absence of noise
is a negative silence

— a positive
silence is different.

17

In everything we do, we need to give our consent.
We cannot go against our self.
Discipline and obedience are
strengtheners for our self,

they are not tests or commands.

They are the early foundations from which
we learn something much stronger,
more resilient, and something
that stays with us forever.

But first, we must give consent
to ourselves.

18

If we do not start with achieving little things, how will we ever move on to achieve the larger goals?

We work on the little things first.

19

The sacred is not only in the still,
small voice that sings inside of you.

It is also in all the voices,
and all the silences, and all the spaces in-between.

Search for it,
and search well.

20

The effort which you make individually will not remain
only upon an individual level
— it will spread out.

It will spread and help all those around you.

Never underestimate the potential within everyone
— within each of you.

Self-discipline is indispensable to you
as an individual — it allows you
to be free from the discipline
imposed upon you from others in life.

This freedom we can then share
with those around us,
who need it also.

21

Each thing has its own nature.

Each thing can be discovered
for what it truly is
— just like the flower.

Flowers
are the
spontaneous expression
of the sacred.

Flowers teach us their charm,
like a wordless prayer
— there is a special speech
in silence.

22

We carry the deep unconsciousness
within us,
within our bodies,
our memories,

just as the earth
carries it in her minerals

and her stones.

23

Each of us should struggle against remaining fixed,
stuck in our slice of jellied life,

like an insect preserved
in precious stone.

24

All takes time,
that's the natural way of things.

Everything takes time
to create, time to happen.

25

The practice of going inward
is an aspect of the feminine.

Nurture it as the soil
nurtures her living beings.

Going outward is a sign
of the world.

Going inward is a mark
of the soul.

26

Things may not appear fair or just
on the outside,
but everything finds its balance.

Things which may appear in
contradiction are often working together
— just like the sun and the rain,
and the light and the dark.

It is within the darkness
where the hidden ways of creation
can be found.

27

Life is given for a purpose

and our task

is to find that purpose

and carry out our agreed task.

28

There is a deep unknowing that resides within us,
slumbering and yet watchful

— waiting for our moments
of attentiveness
so that it may awaken
a little more.

29

You already contain the essence;
you cannot develop upon this,

but you can allow it to
unfold and spread out

in the most correct
and harmonious way.

30

What goes on inside of you will spread out.

Transformation is contagious:

Be the positive virus

31

We are here to play the game —

it is important to know that we are
supported in this game by a great amount of energy.

Most people do not suspect the game exists
— this is the sad part.
If there's no game, there's no play.

Yet for those who know, the question becomes
how to play.

It is not a 'normal' game
- it is far more precious, and exhilarating.

We must learn this game,
and to act deliberately.

This is the game that we call Life.

32

One should not fight or struggle against silence.

We are here to cultivate
the art of listening
to silence.

To obtain an attentive silence
is both a delicate

and yet a most practical
and important skill.

33

Each person has a space
where all things of the outer world
do not stir.

It is a space within the self
that is both deeply still and
yet active at the same time.

It is a space that knows no contradiction
and where the flame of knowing
burns as bright as running water.

Each person must seek
and find this space
for themselves.

34

Do not seek perfection

but learn to work
with the frailties.

No one begins from
completion

— it is a destination and not a starting point.

35

We have to bring back things
from the unseen to the seen,
from non-activity to activity

By making things active
you make them alive in the world.

The softest can overcome the hardest;
the subtlest can transform the coarsest.

The light within one awakens
the light within another

— this is the transmission.

36

We each must work with our promises
 — when we give a promise
it must be accomplished.

Treat your words as if they were your children.

37

One must listen to the feeling of assent
we have within each of us.

It is a subtle feeling inside the chest,
near the solar plexus.

It also shows us when something is
against the essential self.

We can feel its assent;
likewise, we can feel its silent voice
when it speaks out against our actions and thoughts.

It is a lighthouse that shines no light,
and yet guides us.

38

The shadows of doubt are not necessarily
bad for us.

They can help us define the light of the truth.
They show to us the obstacles that are placed
in our path.

They provide contrasts, and it is from these
that we can see clearly where the light is,
where it is not,

and those places which
lack the *essential*.

39

Do not concern yourself with the faults of others:

observe them, and then allow this reflection
to come back upon yourself.

Recognition of our own self
comes from the recognition of others.

Trust in yourself,
and what you
represent.

40

We are all fools

— yet some of us

are conscious fools.

41

Never doubt that the energy from the web of life
surges through you -
remember you are always deeply connected.

However, it is crucial to make the energy collective.

If we keep what we have, each for ourselves,
then it will not work for you.

We must offer ourselves in service
- offering ourselves is the only way of keeping
the energy going.

We must give a part of ourselves.

Then you are going to start to feel
connected to something that will
forever guide your actions.

The deeper you connect, the more knowing comes.

42

There is nothing nobler
than the inward recognition
of two souls.

43

Where there is no harmony
there is no possibility
for engaging with
the essential.

It is as simple as that.

Harmony is what brings things together
into a correct alignment

It lies inside each one of us,
and also operates between us.

If there is no harmony
we can do almost nothing.

Trust in this.

44

Life is more than just a hall of mirrors

- it is a sparklehorse
of splintered fragments

each showing an image
of the whole.

45

We are each working
towards something that is
greater than any one of us.

In this life we need gifts.

Without gifts we are unable
to move forward.

You being here now
is one of those gifts.

46

The genuine expression of truth

takes no fixed form.

47

Everything you do
is in recognition of
where *you* are.

We are here to compel change upon others.

48

Those things which are seemingly in opposition
are often working in harmony.

Behind the appearance of contradictions
often lies the greater truth of conciliation.

This harmony, this working in unison,
creates another force
— the force of transformation.

Goodwill alone is not an effective force
for transformation.

A conscious intent and personal power
are required,

to be applied in the right way
and when necessary.

49

If you run away from this world
and from your responsibilities within it

you leave open a space
for adverse forces to rush in.

Do not let them in.

Likewise,
do not oppose negative forces
with weakness.

It's like blowing
on a flower
- you only serve to further spread its seeds.

50

You are *here*.

It's always about
where *you* are.

Everything has to come through you
— has to work through you.

We are each of us as a book
that doesn't need to be
read aloud.

Wisdom is not in the pages of a book
but in your presence.

And people will read you
in many varied ways.

51

The deeper the darkness in the world
the more light that is needed.

Some of this light is provided by the sun,
and is reflected here upon the earth.

There is another light which comes from deep within us
— a light that shines from a different star.

There is a responsibility to bring
this greater light into the world,
into our everyday life.

The unfolding begins deep
within us like a seed.

52

We can allow
ourselves to be engulfed
by the Great Mystery.

And then,
once we have been engulfed,
we have to be willing
to be dismantled,
again and again,
so that we finally go beyond
who we think we are.

Then shall we have the ability
to be both present and absent.

To be present in this world,
yet also able to shift into *another place*,

allows one to tune into what
needs to be done here in the everyday.

53

If you are not truly sincere
with yourself
then you can't make it.

There will be obstacles
that keep presenting themselves,

and only sincerity

will clear the way.

Through the vessel of sincerity
flows love.

54

If you work just for yourself, you limit yourself.

You must allow yourself
to be used by that

which has no name

and yet

knows all names.

Something larger contains the smaller
— the greater is
but the outward face

of the essence.

55

Consistency and persistence...

ignorance is not cured by adopting
the easiest methods.

56

The act of giving
has benefit
in accordance
with the
consciousness

of the giver.

57

Essence is a sacred,
living transmission
with no religious building,
formal structure,
or earthly institution

- it is transmitted through
the hearts and minds of people.

When people are gathered together,
or in correspondence and communion,
they are connected to
the essence which

ensouls the world.

58

Whilst we may act independently
we should not become attached
to our individual effort.

Individual effort is only one
of many means of action.

There are forces that act upon us
and those that act through us;
and these forces have greater power
if we allow our collaboration.

Make your aim
to transmit
without
distortion.

59

The sun doesn't rain
and the moon does not
provide its own light.

Everything *gives* according
to what it can,

and we must approach each and all
according to its capacity
and essential nature.

60

The invisible golden thread
is what has been planted
in our hearts.

Each of us
can bring our part
of the thread
into the whole
tapestry.

From that moment
we contribute
and participate
in the
whole design.

We are each
connected in ways
not visible to others.

We take this with us
when we go out into the world.

Our connection to this golden thread
reminds us constantly that goodness
lies deep within all things
and can be found.

61

We live with questions all our lives,
and yet often fail to notice them
or to awake them from their slumber within us.

People are many things that they themselves
do not know.
They can be blind and not know it
because they are blinded by a light
that makes them

look away.

A gift is but a tool
whose use each person
must choose.

62

The type of energy you choose
to identify with will mark
more than your personality

— it will mark how your future unfolds.

Such paths are not set in stone,
as many wish to believe.

All paths are open and adapt
to circumstances, decisions,
and opportunities taken

as well as those missed.

63

The sacred is not only
in the stillness inside of you
but also in all the spaces in-between.

Seek your own
speechless communion
with the centre
inside of you.

True communion

will be your freedom.

64

The power of silence is a gift.

We can dress ourselves with this beautiful gift
and walk amongst the world
as a true warrior of the heart.

First you must learn to
befriend your silence
— make it your companion.

Your companion is also your personal centre.
It is the place deep within you where
you are always sincere.

It is the place that knows you
better than you know yourself,
and from which you cannot
hide nor lie.

65

You can gain from making the right effort,
but lose from undue force.

Do not hold back, or be afraid,
from making right *effort*.

Those who are afraid, are afraid everywhere —
those who have faith and trust
inside themselves shall be safe,
wherever they go.

66

Do not shy away
from the source of communion
within *you*.

Avoid those things which only
serve to destabilize you or
detract you from your work.

Do not try to appease
those forces that work against you
— move around them.

Do not be timid within yourself.

67

The world binds us to it —
we each of us belong to the world,
yet each in our different ways.

We must learn what
binds us,
and what those binds are

— whether they are chains,
obligations, or willing service.

What binds us can also be
what nurtures us.

In this way
we can *play* the game
rather than being played.

68

Many people are seeking to forget.

We are here to remember
— to not allow ourselves to forget.

To be attentive
to life.

This is our duty.

It is our responsibility
to act upon the
ignorance of others.

69

Delight is
the secret that lies
hidden behind everything
you see in this
world.

70

You don't talk to people

about recipes

when you know

they suffer from hunger.

71

You already contain the essence,
you cannot develop upon this;

but you can allow it to unfold
and spread out in the most correct
and harmonious way.

72

Humanity,
in its natural state,
seeks to be
in harmony
with its world.

73

Play the game.
Play for that which is bigger than you.

Play for that part of yourself that knows
there is a reason for being here.

Play for all those *togethers* that unite into one.

Play for the stars, the heavens, and everything
that ever existed.

If you don't play for the evermore,
then you are just playing your
own little game.

And then it's your own little world.
And all your meanings will stop once
the game finishes.

Play the game with reverence

— with love.

74

You will not be empty by giving.

You will be filled, restored,
so that you have
more to give.

Do not be that person
who unknowingly takes
away from others.

Your role is to provide for others,
for those that do not
know or suspect.

75

Be like a fugitive in this world
— an inside outsider

who holds the cup full
of deepest and sweetest
appreciation and gratitude.

76

Work with the
four hands of

patience,
compassion,
understanding,

and doing

the little things.

77

The light
within each atom
will shine because
of what you do.

78

We operate within the body of the world

and we are known only by our exterior faces.

Yet *we* recognize each other.

79

Where there is no harmony
— no grace —

there is
no true
correspondence.

80

We can each reflect back
the transcendence
that lies at the heart
of the cosmos.

81

Whenever you reach a plateau,
a greater effort is required to push past it.

Otherwise, one remains marooned
upon their own island,
content to think that the end
has been reached

when one is still adrift.

82

We each have
a golden thread
within us

that is the
timelessness

out of which

the cosmos is

ceaselessly born.

83

Growing old is only

the flakes that fall
from an outer skin.

We always were
and
always shall be.

84

Each human being
is like the seed of a flower,

awaiting

to pollinate in the world.

85

If something new enters
then something old must leave.
There always has to be a harmony.

As there is breath in,
there is breath out

— the inhale, the exhale.

86

Sacrifice is
everything and nothing

- it is the
radiant heart
and the
receptive womb.

It is how the cosmos loves,
and to sacrifice

is the greatest love.

87

Some things just *are*...

The rest is waiting
— waiting until the already known
becomes conscious.

Everything has its need,
and such needs
have their time.

The human heart reflects
the purposeful patterns
of the cosmos.

89

Be tireless, be loving
- be the true feminine
of this earth.

There is nothing greater,
more beautiful,
or more fulfilling.

90

For you are

the sun,
the moon,
the rain,
and the
heartbeat.

You are everything and you are nothing.

You are of the soil and of the spirit.

Embrace all,
and be
embraced by all.

Leave nothing untouched.

Books deserving...
for inquiring minds......

Beautiful Traitor Books was founded in 2012 as an independent print-on-demand imprint to provide unusual and inspiring books for the discerning reader.

Our books are works that delve into various domains whether it is books for children, science fiction, social affairs, philosophy, theatre plays, or poetry. All the books we publish seek to explore innovative and creative ideas. Many of them also tell a good story - stories that have different perspectives on life and on the human condition.

Beautiful Traitor Books is not only about offering the reader entertainment. We also seek to offer something that is like a nutrition; something of value that the reader can take away from the book. Good books function on more than one level. Put simply, we thrive on books that have the capacity to *shift* the reader.

Come and join the conversation – find out more at: www.beautifultraitorbooks.com

www.ingramcontent.com/pod-product-compliance
Lightning Source LLC
Chambersburg PA
CBHW061120070526
44583CB00028B/3344